OLD ENOUGH to SAVE the PLANET

written by **Loll Kirby**
illustrated by **Adelina Lirius**
foreword by **Kallan Benson**

MAGIC CAT PUBLISHING

NEW YORK

Calling all activists!

Hi, I'm Kallan.

At nine, I started to worry about climate change and the future, but I didn't know what I could do. Marching in the first Peoples Climate March changed my life. I was surrounded by art and funny signs. People were dancing, playing instruments, singing, and chanting. I realized that I already had skills that could help change the world. Anything I could do would contribute.

Through Parachutes for the Planet with the Mother Earth Project, I have worked with thousands of kids all around the world who use art with their friends and families to explore and share concerns about the future. Now, I am helping to build the global climate strike community with FridaysforFuture. Greta Thunberg says, "You are never too small to make a difference." I say, "Everyone is a changemaker." Your work starts with those around you. I can't wait to see how you change the world for the better.

Kallan Benson,
Cofounder of FridaysforFuture

In this book, meet twelve
real-life children . . .

Felix from Germany

Passionate reforestation activist and
creator of Plant-for-the-Planet

Hunter from South Africa

Campaigner for the protection of rhinos
against the threat of poachers

Nikita from Ukraine

Responsible for turning his school's
food waste into usable compost for
his home city

Himangi from India

Campaigner for reducing the effects
of traffic pollution outside her school

Amy and Ella from the UK

Two sisters committed to eradicating
single-use plastic through their charity
Kids Against Plastic

Adeline from Indonesia

Reintroduced native species of plants
and animals after severe floods
affected her home

Brooklyn from Georgia, USA

Young writer who visits schools around her
country to talk about the effects of trash

Vincent from France

Creator of a community garden
that reduces food waste

Eunita from Kenya

Founder of a community garden that
promotes the natural process of pollination

Shalise from Australia

Protects the ocean by cleaning
up trash from the shore

Jordan from New York, USA

Spokesperson for the responsible use
of palm oil products to reduce the
destruction of rainforests

The children at Hengde School, China

Built a water ecological learning
field to learn about water
conservation and ecology

I'm big enough to save our trees . . .

Felix, from Germany, was concerned about the vast numbers of trees being cut down all over the world. When he was nine years old, he launched Plant-for-the-Planet to get schoolchildren all around the world to join together and plant new trees in their own countries. His idea was so successful that a few years later, more than one million trees had been planted in nearly one hundred countries.

A huge number of trees are cut down around the world every day.

Trees are cut down to make room for farmland and housing or to harvest the wood.

Trees of all shapes and sizes form a vital part of the habitats of many of the world's creatures.

Humans take in oxygen from the air and get rid of carbon dioxide, but trees do the opposite. Without them, we wouldn't be able to breathe.

Felix adds the last bits of soil around a tree he's just planted.

NAME: Felix Finkbeiner

COUNTRY: Germany

CHANGEMAKER FOR: Global reforestation

I'm resourceful enough to reduce traffic pollution . . .

If everybody uses a car, traffic jams build up quickly in areas with lots of homes and workplaces.

People can get hurt trying to move safely among the vehicles, and accidents can happen.

Walking and cycling are great ways to reduce both air pollution and the amount of traffic on the road.

The traffic outside Himangi's school in India became such a problem that the nine-year-old took action and started a campaign to encourage people to cycle instead of drive.

She also organized better places for cars and rickshaws to wait so that children could leave school safely. Other local schools were so impressed with her ideas that they started using them as well.

SCHOOL

The exhaust fumes given off by cars, vans, and trucks create air pollution, which can cause health problems.

Himangi waves goodbye to her friends as she walks home from school.

In some towns and cities, air pollution can get so bad that scientists say it isn't safe for people to go outside.

NAME: Himangi Halder
COUNTRY: India
CHANGEMAKER FOR:
Reducing the effects of traffic pollution

We're smart enough to stop buying single-use plastic . . .

Bigger plastic items like bottles end up in landfill sites.

KIDS against PLASTIC

After learning about the negative effects of plastic waste, British sisters Amy, sixteen, and Ella, fourteen, set up a charity to share their knowledge and get people involved in their work. They inform others about how we can replace single-use plastic bottles with reusable alternatives. They've created a website with lots of useful resources, as well as an app to track plastic litter, and they've persuaded many schools, businesses, and city councils to make positive changes in how they use plastic.

Lots of plastic items can easily be swapped for more environmentally friendly alternatives, like using beeswax wrap instead of plastic wrap to keep food fresh.

PLASTIC IN THE OCEAN

Much smaller plastic items such as microbeads—found in things like shampoo—can end up in the ocean and be swallowed by fish, making them sick.

PARK CLEANUP

Amy and Ella explain how a reusable bottle is so much better than a plastic one.

Amy

Ella

Many everyday items are made from plastic, but they can be difficult to recycle.

Some plastic items might not even need a replacement. More and more supermarkets are selling loose products with no packaging, and customers fill up their own jars and bags to take them home.

NAME: Amy and Ella Meek

COUNTRY: UK

CHANGEMAKER FOR: The elimination of single-use plastics

I'm powerful enough to preserve the environment . . .

Flooding was wreaking havoc in Indonesia, where Adeline lives, as a result of humans destroying the natural environment. At the age of twelve, she formed a community group called Friends of Nature to address the cause of these disasters. She organized people to replant the native mangrove trees that had been cut down and to create protected areas in the sea to allow new coral reefs to form. She also spent time educating others about the impact that human activity has on the world around us.

Cutting down trees means that rainwater can flow freely over the land and become a flood.

Changing the natural environment can have serious consequences for plants, animals, and humans.

Biodiversity is a word to describe having a wide variety of plants and animals in any given habitat, which is very important for keeping our environment healthy.

Dumping toxic waste in the ocean can cause coral reefs to die away.

Adeline supports a newly planted tree with a cane.

Overfishing can destroy the biodiversity of our oceans.

NAME: Adeline Tiffanie Suwana
COUNTRY: Indonesia
CHANGEMAKER FOR:
Biodiversity and the reintroduction of native plant species

I'm compassionate enough
to protect animals . . .

Rhinos are a critically endangered species, which means they are at an extremely high risk of extinction.

Hunter spends time with the rhinos he has helped to rescue.

When a species becomes extinct, it means that there are no more of them left alive in the wild.

When he found out about an abandoned baby rhino, Hunter donated his pocket money to help the people looking after it, even though he was only seven at the time.

He persuaded lots of other people in his home country, South Africa, to give money toward caring for rhinos as well. He now talks to people all over the world about how important it is to look after all wildlife and prevent endangered species from becoming extinct.

Rhinos are being hunted because people want to take their horns.

Some of these people believe that rhino horns are useful for making medicines, while others think they are a sign of wealth and success.

Some people are so eager to get rhino horns that they kill the rhinos illegally, which is called poaching.

NAME: Hunter Mitchell
COUNTRY: South Africa
CHANGEMAKER FOR: Protecting endangered species

I'm creative enough to stamp out litter . . .

Brooklyn, from Georgia, was seven years old when she wrote a book called *The Adventures of Earth Saver Girl* **to teach people about why litter is a problem.** She visits schools to talk about her book and entertains children with songs and plays to show that saving the environment can also be fun.

Litter is a problem that most of us encounter every day. We might see food wrappers dropped in the streets or spot old bottles floating in the river.

Litter spoils how our environment looks but it can also damage the plants and animals that live around us if it doesn't biodegrade.

When something biodegrades, it decays naturally over time and is absorbed by the environment without causing it any harm.

Synthetic materials like plastic, some rubber, and nylon can take many hundreds of years to disappear completely, so litter containing items made of these is a much bigger problem.

Natural materials like food waste will biodegrade completely within a few months.

EARTH SAVER GIRL

Brooklyn is dressed up as Earth Saver Girl, encouraging her friends to join her!

NAME: Brooklyn Wright
COUNTRY: USA
CHANGEMAKER FOR:
Reducing litter pollution

I'm inspired enough to eat locally grown food . . .

Many larger farms spray chemicals on their plants to help them grow, as well as to kill weeds and insects.

Growing food close to where it will be eaten means that it doesn't have to be transported a long way in refrigerated trucks or airplanes (these vehicles use fuels that harm our environment).

Organic farms don't use chemicals on their plants and rely on natural methods to keep their crops healthy.

Vincent, an eleven-year-old from France, recognized the environmental impact of large-scale farming and secured funding to set up an organic community garden in his village.

He believed this would encourage his friends and neighbors to consider food production more carefully and to take some responsibility for how their food was grown. His project has been very successful and has now expanded to include a beehive and a greenhouse. It has also brought people in his community closer together.

Eating fresh food that has recently been picked avoids the need for lots of packaging and storage and reduces food waste.

If you've grown your own food, you know that it will taste good in any shape or size.

Vincent picks an apple from a tree in his garden

NAME: Vincent Depaire
COUNTRY: France
CHANGEMAKER FOR: Organic gardening as a way to produce food and reduce waste

I know enough to save the bees . . .

Nine-year-old Eunita learned about the importance of pollination while visiting an ancient forest in Kenya, where she lives. Her trip inspired her to create a garden near her home that would attract bees and other creatures that help to spread pollen. She has put up signs in her town to explain her work to her community, and she sells seeds to help other people start their own gardens.

When a bee drinks nectar, the pollen from the flower sticks to the bee's legs. This bee then carries the pollen to the next flower.

Bees like to live in areas filled with wildflowers, grasses, and trees.

BEES

SUNBIRDS

Without this pollen new plants can't grow, including those that provide food for us to eat.

Bees' habitats are being destroyed so humans can use the land for other things, leaving the bees homeless.

Eunita prepares to plant some wildflowers that will attract bees.

NAME: Eunita Atitwa
COUNTRY: Kenya
CHANGEMAKER FOR:
The preservation of bees and education of people about pollinators

All around the world, a huge amount of food waste is taken to landfill sites every day.

One way to reduce food waste is to take suitable leftovers, such as bread crusts or apple cores, and find a way to turn them into compost.

I'm responsible enough to make use of our food waste . . .

Nikita, a twelve-year-old from Ukraine, decided to make use of the food waste that was being thrown away at his school. Along with a friend, he set up a project to separate food leftovers from other types of trash, and then turn them into compost that could be used to nourish the city's plants and trees. Their work was so successful that many other schools around the country have adopted the idea and are using their waste to create their own compost.

This compost eventually becomes a nutrient-rich fertilizer, which can be used to help new plants and trees grow.

Compost is made by allowing organic materials such as leaves, twigs, and food waste to slowly decompose.

Nikita empties a bucket of fruit and vegetable peelings into the school compost bin.

Compost can be made on a large scale in schools or restaurants, or on a smaller scale at home.

NAME: Nikita Shulga
COUNTRY: Ukraine
CHANGEMAKER FOR: Diverting food waste from landfill into compost projects

I care enough to clean up the ocean . . .

Shalise was eleven years old when she started working to clean up the ocean near where she lives in Australia. She goes down to the beach every weekend to tidy up and make notes on the garbage she finds. She also got her local council to provide special bins for old fishing lines and to put up signs explaining how we can take better care of marine animals and their habitat.

DUMP OLD FISHING LINE HERE

Fishing lines are very dangerous for marine animals, who can get tangled up in them and become seriously injured.

It's not just beaches that need cleaning up—trash from people living inland can find its way out to sea after it ends up in a river that flows into the ocean.

Trash is destroying the world's coral reefs, making them more vulnerable to diseases that damage their health.

It takes hundreds of years for fishing lines and other trash to break down and disappear, so it causes a lot of damage if it isn't cleaned up.

Shalise explains to her friend why it's important to collect trash from the beach.

There are now many garbage patches in our oceans and the largest of these, the Great Pacific Patch, is about the size of Texas—but it is hard to get an accurate measurement.

NAME: Shalise Leesfield
COUNTRY: Australia
CHANGEMAKER FOR:
Rescuing the ocean
from being destroyed
by pollution

I'm clever enough to look for palm oil alternatives . . .

Jordan, an eleven-year-old from New York, became concerned about the use of palm oil while doing research for a school project on orangutans.
He discovered that rainforests that are home to orangutans were being burned down to make space to grow more oil palms. He contacted lots of companies that used palm oil in their products to ask them to say so clearly on their labels so that more people would be aware of the issue. He also set up a website to share his work and encourage others to help.

Rainforests are home to a huge number of plant and animal species—so many, in fact, that we haven't even discovered most of them!

A large number of everyday food and beauty products contain palm oil, from soap and shampoo to chocolate and bread.

Jordan hands a banana to an orangutan who happily plays in its rainforest home.

The smoke that results from burning down the rainforests contains carbon dioxide and other pollutants, which can cause serious pollution problems.

Burning down the rainforest to grow more oil palm trees means that lots of species—including orangutans—could die out forever.

Palm oil isn't bad in itself, but we need to be much more careful about how and where it is produced, as well as how companies use it.

NAME: Jordan Salama
COUNTRY: USA
CHANGEMAKER FOR:
Raising awareness about the impact of palm oil

We're dedicated enough to save water . . .

Humans cannot survive without water, so there is more demand for it as the world's population grows.

Freshwater shortages affect one in three people around the world, mainly in developing countries.

At Hengde, the children are learning how a spray nozzle on the end of a tap can slow water flow and reduce waste.

The children at Hengde Primary School in China wanted to find ways to make their school more environmentally friendly. They worked together to create an ecological field on their school grounds that educated students about water conservation through games and other activities. Their most important achievement was finding a way to adapt their drainage system so that waste water could be used to irrigate the small farm areas outside each classroom. All their ideas have been useful, and they are still working to find more.

Climate change is leading to rising global temperatures that may lead to more droughts, making it even more important to conserve water as much as possible.

Whether in school or at home, you can reduce water waste, scraping leftovers and removing grease before washing your plate.

NAME: Hengde Primary School

COUNTRY: China

CHANGEMAKER FOR:
Teaching others about water ecology and conservation

How can you help to save the planet?

In 2016, the Intergovernmental Panel on Climate Change (IPCC) investigated the issue of climate change. The IPCC is made up of representatives from many countries, and they worked together to find scientific evidence of climate change. They found that the world is already 34 degrees Fahrenheit warmer than two hundred years ago, when there were no cars or large-scale factories. The IPCC predicts that global warming will reach 35 to 36 degrees Fahrenheit above these preindustrial levels within the next thirty years. Scientists believe we can avoid this if we take action now.

1. Buy products with little or no packaging. Millions of tons of plastic waste enter our oceans each year, and much of this is unnecessary packaging.

2. Stop food waste. Being careful about the food we buy means we will avoid throwing things away because they are moldy or stale. Food waste generates greenhouse gases too!

3. Mend things instead of throwing them away. With certain electronics, for example, 75 to 80 percent of the energy a device uses over its lifetime is spent during manufacturing.

4. Walk, or use public transportation, instead of using a car. Carbon emissions per passenger for trains and buses are about four times lower than for cars.

5. Think carefully before traveling by airplane. About a billion tons of the world's annual carbon emissions come from air travel.

6. Turn off the tap when you're brushing your teeth. A simple but easy way to save water each day.

7. Aim to eat more seasonal, locally grown produce to reduce food miles (the distance food has to travel from where it's grown to where it's eaten). Since 1992, the amount of food flown around the world by airplane has increased by 140 percent. Food that is grown and sold close to where you live will need very little transportation.

8. Eat less meat. Following a meat-free diet results in about half the carbon emissions of a meat-eating diet (defined as eating more than 110 grams of meat a day).

9. Save energy at home wherever possible. Switching off lights when you leave a room and not leaving devices charging overnight saves a lot of energy. You can also use LED lights, which last much longer and are more energy efficient.

10. Buy less stuff! This applies to pretty much everything. To use clothing as an example, hundreds of thousands of tons are put into our trash cans each year.

Ten things you can do to make your voice heard

1. Write to your representatives. You can find out how out how to do this online.

2. Write to your local city officials. They can often help you to make changes in your area.

3. Educate others. If you're not yet. old enough to vote, share your research with those in your family who are.

4. Create a petition. It can be easier to get things done when you have lots of support for the changes you'd like to make.

5. Set up a group of people working toward a similar goal. You could pick a topic you're passionate about and get everyone involved.

6. Write to newspapers, magazines, or websites with your ideas. They can share them widely and get people interested in your plans.

7. Stay up to date with the news. Watch, listen, and read as much as you can to stay informed.

8. Gather friends and family and join a protest. You can make banners and signs to share your thoughts as well.

9. Go on strike Thin is growing in popularity among schoolchildren as a peaceful means of effectively demonstrating to others how strongly you feel.

10. Speak out at every opportunity. Just chatting with people at school or in your family is helpful, and you might learn something new by listening to them as well.

Further Reading

With the help of an adult, find out more about the children and issues featured in this book on these websites:

climatekids.nasa.gov

climaterealityproject.org

earthpeacefoundation.org

earthsavergirl.com

greenpeace.org

kidsagainstpalmoil.org

plant-for-the-planet.org

The illustrations were created in pen and ink and colored digitally.
Set in Rainer and Panforte Pro.

Library of Congress Control Number 2019955017

ISBN 978-1-4197-4914-8

Text copyright © 2020 Magic Cat Publishing
Illustrations copyright © 2020 Adelina Lirius
Written by Loll Kirby
Foreword by Kallan Benson
Designed by Nicola Price

Printed and bound in China using vegetable inks.
10 9 8 7 6

Abrams Books are available at special discounts when purchased in quantity for premiums and promotions as well as fundraising or educational use. Special editions can also be created to specification. For details, contact specialsales@abramsbooks.com or the address below.

ABRAMS The Art of Books
195 Broadway, New York, NY 10007
abramsbooks.com